HERMAN
THE SIXTH TREASURY

HERMAN
THE SIXTH TREASURY

by Jim

Foreword
by Gene Shalit

Andrews and McMeel
A Universal Press Syndicate Company
Kansas City • New York

HERMAN® is syndicated internationally by Universal Press Syndicate.

ISBN: 0-8362-1832-9
Library of Congress Catalog Card Number: 88-71104

First Printing, July 1988
Third Printing, September 1991

Foreword

The highest compliment I can pay to Herman is that he's from Unger. Now, "Jim Unger" would never stoop to such a pun, assuming that there really is a "Jim Unger," which I doubt. I mean, have *you* ever seen him? Me neither. Having laughed uproariously at Herman for so many years, I've concluded that "Jim Unger" is the communal name for a corps of writers and artists who produce these hilarious panels seven days a week, year in, year out, under the command of a comic virtuoso who drives them on with a crack of the quip. Just imagine what a "Jim Unger" would have to be if he were just one person: an inspired humorist, a master of line drawings, an astute student of human behavior and phobias, a keen observer of romantic and domestic relationships, abnormal psychology, emotional disturbances, and body English. He would have the audacity to express thoughts and feelings the rest of us wouldn't dare to say out loud. When Herman felt trapped in a seven-year relationship, he precipitated this conversation:

> He: "How do you feel about running away and getting married?"
> She: "I'd love it."
> He: "Give me a call when you get back."

Not only is Herman not Her Man, he is not *any*body's man. He is one of a kind and of a kind never before seen. He's such a winner because he's such a loser. He is the epitome, the apotheosis, the . . . oh, the heck with it. Herman is Herman, and that's wonderful!

—GENE SHALIT

P.S. The publishers inform me that there really *is* a Jim Unger and that he lives in the Bahamas. Sure.

by Jim Unger

20,000 FEET.

WE'RE 10,000 FEET FROM THE SURFACE, COMMANDER.

PLANET EARTH IS NOW 5,000 FEET BELOW...

STAND BY, 50 FEET

10 FEET

9

"Good grief, it *is* you! How long's it been? Twenty years? I thought I recognized the suit."

"When he was six years old, my father was kidnapped by headhunters and never seen again."

"What do you mean you don't trust banks? You only have $34."

"It says: 'Ideal for first-time home buyers. Only $214,000.'"

"She makes her own clothes!"

"Your resume says you spent 'fore years at collej.'"

"*You're* a vet. Don't *you* know what it is?"

"Your driver's license expired in 1914."

"Thanks for a lovely party last night. I know George had a good time."

"Your hair transplant is being rejected!"

"Take four aspirin and call me in the morning."

"Harold, the doctor made you quit the insurance office because you kept bringing your work home."

"Power steering, of course."

"You arrive at 5 p.m. and your connecting flight leaves at 7 p.m. That leaves you only two hours to clear customs."

"Do you know if you want Dr. Humblestone the skin specialist or Dr. Humblestone the gynecologist?"

"I can guarantee it won't go frizzy with these babies."

"What made you give up your last job as an electrician?"

"All we have is twin, double, and queen-size."

"We're not doing 3,500 miles an hour. That's the tachometer."

"Didn't you pay the cable TV bill?"

"She's not home....Wait for the click...then leave your message."

"Go and open the front door while your mother's cooking. I don't want the fire department breaking it down with an ax."

"Mother, I wish you wouldn't rent those old disco movies."

"How's the water?"

"I'm sorry, but a snapshot of you
at Niagara Falls is not my idea
of proper identification."

"Visiting hours don't start
'til 2 o'clock, Angela. I'm
surprised they let you in."

"When are you people going
to get that elevator fixed?"

"Yes, we know what it is. We want to know where you got it!"

"We're always looking for bright, young, intelligent guys like you."

"Is this 38 miles on the odometer genuine?"

"Here, I found your glasses in the kitchen."

"Susan, I won't be prepared to be a grandmother for at least another 15 years."

"Is that how you like your coffee?"

"Do you fancy some of
this leftover stew?"

"He was on a one-day strike at
work today and nobody noticed."

"Couldn't you hear
that phone ringing?"

"Is this the 54-year-
old limbo dancer?"

"I told you we should have
had the driveway paved."

"I thought you were
going to mow the lawn."

"I told you not to drink
that on an empty stomach."

"Listen, I'd better go. My wife's
waiting to use the phone."

"I'm here on a student
exchange program."

"He's trying to hatch
some duck eggs."

"The doctor says you'll probably be in *The Guinness Book of World Records.*"

"There's just no pleasing you, is there? All week you've been telling me to get a haircut."

"I didn't have the time to get you any flowers."

"I'm not going to give you a tip. I don't like to hurt people's feelings."

"He painted this one while
he was locked in his studio."

"Fill 'er up."

"I want my apple back."

"Luckily, our honeymoon suite
had a TV in the bedroom."

"Why don't you leave the ring and
I'll phone you with my answer."

"Same as yesterday: one sausage,
four french fries, and 11 peas."

"Stick your tongue out.
I want to clean my glasses."

"There's someone out here
waiting to use the phone."

"I always wear my lucky
hat for job interviews."

"Two round-the-world cruises
in opposite directions."

"Are you gonna be able to afford a car
by the time I need to borrow it?"

"Just put it back on the wall."

"We're going to Italy for
a week on his overtime pay."

HERMAN
by Jim Unger

GET A MOVE ON...

DON'T JUST SIT THERE STARING INTO SPACE...CLEAN UP THIS MESS.

I DON'T KNOW WHY YOU CAN'T DO ANYTHING WITHOUT BEING TOLD TWICE.

HOW MUCH LONGER ARE YOU GOING TO SHAKE THAT TABLECLOTH?

"I thought you *liked* shepherd's pie!"

"She's been trying to lower inflation with my credit card."

"I usually have to drive him home after a party."

"I was rubbing two sticks together and discovered first-degree burns."

"I can't bring the car
back 'til low tide."

"I need 148 get-well cards."

"We're planning a second honeymoon
if I can get an hour off work."

"Four blocks north. If it's
not there, eight blocks south."

"I rolled the car on the way to band practice."

"I know there's a full moon tonight. Don't keep thinking about it."

"You've got exactly 15 seconds to start putting up that wallpaper in our bedroom."

"I'm not worried about *his* future. We were only in the park 10 minutes."

"How many times have I told
you not to call me at work?"

"Can't you make less
noise when you eat?"

"You put the comics page in here.
You know he likes the editorials."

"Will you *please* ask your mother
to sit over on my side?"

"I just found out your lawyer specializes in real estate."

"Don't creep around. I heard the garage door three minutes ago."

"Your doctor wants to marry me if you don't make it."

"Don't keep saying, 'I wonder what it tastes like'!"

"Now that you've cut off my electricity, how do you expect me to find my checkbook in the dark?"

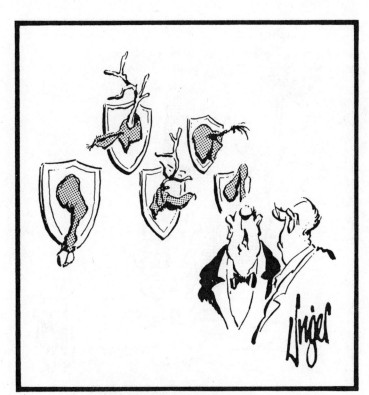

"I hit it with the truck."

"OK, you can stop signaling now."

"I didn't know how to tell you before.
The dog ran off 14 years ago."

"Today's special is all the caviar
you can eat for $600."

"She can say 'charge it'
in 14 languages."

"I think I'll give it a shot
on my own today, Bernie."

"Fifteen seconds away
from a peaceful night."

"Did you lock the *back* door?"

"Of *course* they disqualified you!
You cut across the parking lot."

"Vertical stripes definitely
make you look slimmer."

"I *know* the tablecloth's dirty. Don't forget, this place has been open since 1963."

"How many times have I told you *not* to starch my shirts?"

"Your boss wants to hear you cough."

"He makes $35 an hour as an electrician."

"The airline lost my luggage again."

"Pull up to the front of that apartment building and leave the engine running."

"They haven't built the crib that can hold me."

"I've got to get some new curtains for the living room. Where did you hide the $6 million?"

"If you order the chili, I need
to know your next-of-kin."

"Open this up exactly halfway between
Christmas and your birthday."

"That's the big clock in the kitchen."

"Don't ask."

"Go past a steakhouse, turn right at the doughnut shop, then keep going until you see a fish and chip place opposite two pizza parlors. If you come to Harry's Hamburger Joint you've gone too far."

"Don't mess around. I know where you are."

"O'Reilly, did you leave this junk on my desk?"

"To be honest, I'd heard
you'd gone abroad."

"He's got his grandfather's nose."

"You're being released. Be ready
to leave in 30 minutes."

"Keep your mouth closed
when you're eating."

"You just plug it in once a month."

"I wouldn't be able to see a thing if she hadn't had her ears pierced."

"Listen, I've got to go. That guy's still hanging around waiting to use the phone."

"He moved!"

"I'll have two eggs
and some b-a-c-o-n."

"Did you advertise for an experienced
salesman in ladies underwear?"

"He fell off the corporate ladder when
he asked for the minimum wage."

"How could *anyone* flush
a goldfish down a sink?"

"Get down, Robert. Remember
you're an accountant."

49

"You don't get atmosphere like this watching it on television."

"I bought the first cup last Tuesday."

"I did quite a bit of painting in the hospital."

"Don't use that thing. I'll get the spray."

"Every time you take him
for a walk he gets longer!"

"He's been at the video rental
store all afternoon, doctor."

"She needs wider skis."

"Nurse!"

"He says fitness is a state of mind. So he sits there thinking about exercise."

"Okay, rinse."

"You're not getting enough Vitamin C."

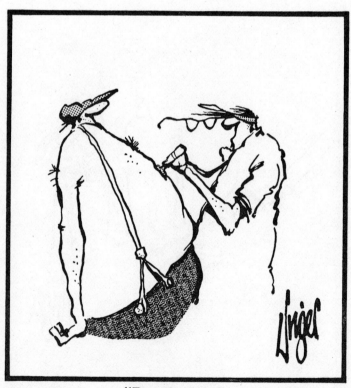

"Breathe out."

"Couldn't he wait?"

"Her idea of a balanced diet is four pounds of chocolate with four pounds of cake."

"I told you you were putting on weight."

"I'm waiting to hear you wipe your feet!"

"You can get in the bathroom now."

"I've put a towel for your mother in here and I'll use the bathroom downstairs."

"Good evening. I'm Andre, your Heimlich Maneuver specialist."

"I don't need anything, dear. I'll stay in bed until the fever dies down."

54

"Don't *nag*. If you want
the light out, say so!"

"Non-smoking unless you're
expecting turbulence."

"This guy wants to know
if we deliver to Africa."

"I usually leave an extra $10
in my pocket on her birthday."

"This is my rent check. Make sure
it circles the globe a few times."

"My husband will be
doing all the parking."

"How are you feeling?"

"I told you not to order
a Zombie in here."

"Your wife says you stopped
a runaway horse."

"Cradle snatcher!"

"Read the instructions very,
very, very, very carefully."

"I am an equal opportunity employer.
That's why I've decided to give
all the other employers an equal
opportunity at your services."

"Hold it! Hold it! My whole life
is flashing before my eyes."

"There's a $100 bill in here!"

"None of those buildings
used to be there."

"Does that hurt?"

"How can you tell if an uncut
diamond is genuine?"

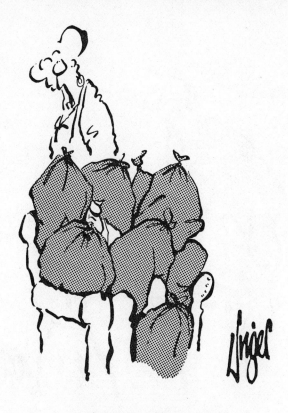

"Don't forget to take
out the garbage."

"I caught it in a copier machine."

"The elephant fainted and
we can't find the keeper."

"Is that the bill for my credit card?"

"Will you please take this thing away from him. I'm *trying* to read."

"If you get straight A's at school, I'll buy you the machine gun."

"I am well aware that it's a religious holiday. But you can't deduct Christmas expenses from your taxes."

"You know Christmas is the only chance Daddy gets to sleep in."

"Guess which tree my dad hit."

"Rambo…Robert…Michael."

"You left this refrigerator
open again."

"There's a girl here who's
been left $100 million! Why
don't you give her a call?"

"And don't wish me a Happy New Year because I *don't* want one."

"You've heard of 'The Battle of the Bulge.' Well, you lost."

"He asked me to put some ketchup in here."

"Well, I just hope I look as good as you do on *my* 110th birthday."

"Nervous flier.... He promised me an extra 10 bucks if I miss his plane."

"Who's having the raw herring?"

"I'm outside the railway station after 3 o'clock."

"The other scraper!"

"Shakespeare, did your father
help you with this homework?"

"I thought you liked this perfume!"

"She never wants to go out."

"Hey, Harry, can I have
the key to the sugar?"

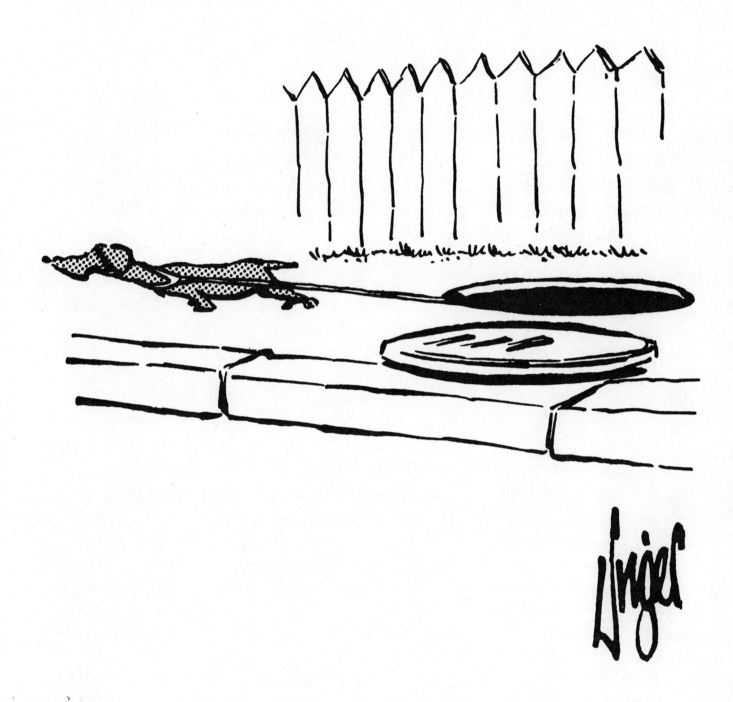

by Jim Unger

NOW WATCH THIS!

THIS IS WHAT WE CALL A "HIGH FLY BALL."

IT CAN BE CAUGHT, BUT IT TAKES CONCENTRATION AND COURAGE.

GET USED TO THE FACT THAT IT LOOKS FIFTY TIMES BIGGER THAN IT REALLY IS ...

CONCENTRATE...

"You know better than to make
a bed like *that*, nurse."

"There's never a bus
when you want one."

"Who's next?"

"My new underwater
watch has stopped!"

"Doctor, I'm not getting a pulse."

"He told me to wake him
at exactly 8 o'clock."

"Good luck, Miller. Try
to stay out of trouble."

"Try to remember all the things
you've eaten in the past three days."

"What time did he discharge himself?"

"You don't want us to become extinct, do you?"

"How much do unemployed veterans usually tip?"

"Don't keep ducking."

"George is an astronomer."

"Now, what seems to
be the trouble?"

"Sure, come over to dinner one
evening. You can have mine."

"D'you want 'Outpatients'
or 'Emergency'?"

"Come along, dear. Daddy's not supposed to go home today."

"We used to fight when we were young. We grew out of it."

"For crying out loud ... it's a mirror!"

"They're gonna use your X-rays in a textbook!"

"Is that supposed to be a tip?"

"Now don't you start that sales resistance stuff — I've had a rough day."

"We handle hi-fi stereo, sir. You need a blacksmith."

"We'd love to have you over for dinner, but we only have nine chairs."

"You guys are too early...
he's not in here yet."

"Got anything for vine-burn?"

"Who am I? And what
am I doing here?"

"Just follow the blue line until
you find your insurance card."

"It's nothing to worry about. You just need to drink more water."

"They finally gave me the key to the executive washroom."

"You shouldn't carry all this cash. Why don't you open an account?"

"Oh, no! Right over the old ladies' home!"

"How much do I have in my account?"

"You'll strain your eyes looking for a job that close!"

"His doctor told him to get some mountain air."

"Did you ask about getting me a bigger room?"

"It *is* an emergency! The potatoes are burning my head."

"If you want a good runabout, buy this.... It won't start."

"You must be the Notorious Captain Phillips."

"Don't keep shouting 'call the plumber.' I've called the plumber."

"I'm not break-dancing! I hit my hand."

"So you were three days into the mountains, then what happened?"

"Can we discuss salary first? My wife's waiting to go shopping."

"I said, take the *lock* off!"

"I take it we're turning right."

"I'm the dishwasher out back.
Hide my tip in the gravy."

"They found your other ski."

"There goes 20 bucks' worth
of fireworks."

"Nurse, can we get
some chairs over here?!"

"You can have that
three-legged one for $7.50."

"It must be your pronunciation.
Let me try."

"We've got to wait for the
shock to wear off. He nearly
drove off an 800-foot cliff."

"What do you mean you
overslept? That's the third
battle you missed this month!"

"Did your mother say you could
build a nuclear device?"

"Two years is a long
time to have jet lag."

"You've had a triple bypass."

"I told you never to get between
Mother and a dessert trolley."

"It's $500, but that includes a
month's supply of breath mints."

"Good news and bad news. The good
news is he won't be scratching
your furniture anymore."

"Just because it's your
turn to change his diaper!"

"Ask him where he left his
key to the safe-deposit box."

"It's for you, Mildred."

89

"You're supposed to
let wine breathe."

"Don't kill it! It'll fly
away on its own."

"If you can spare five seconds,
I'd like to do a brain scan."

PLEASE
WAIT
TO BE
TOLERATED

"In time of war, they could
drop you behind enemy lines
with that frying pan."

"I've gotta get a sample
of your stomach acid."

"If you're *that* worried about catching
it, sleep in the stupid kitchen."

"I've been elected to the
Credit Card Hall of Fame."

"Whadd'yer mean 'the oil's only lukewarm'? They'll be attacking in 10 minutes!"

"What's all this? It says he was born in *three* different places."

"Yes, it's usually been my experience that women go for the type of guy who insists they pay for half of everything."

"Coward!"

"Whadd'yer mean 'He's gone to lunch'?"

"I'm putting this one through law school. He'll get you out."

"He's not house-trained, but who cares?"

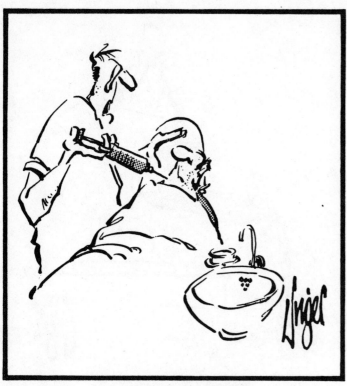

"I can't find my glasses,
so keep still."

"Looks like they hit
the supply wagon."

"Muriel, I want her *out* of the car."

"What is he ever going to
need to know about algebra?
Stick to this country."

"I love you too, sweetheart,
but I've gotta go."

"OK, let's start from where
I told you I needed a man
who could use his head."

"Chest, fifteen and three-quarters."

"Please don't hide your face,
Bellamy. I want to see you in
my office as soon as you get to
the bank tomorrow morning."

"Don't bother to leave a tip.
I had one of your sausages."

"Oh, great! I give you $50 for your
birthday and you spend $5,000."

"Three coffees to go.
Here's the address."

"You *again!*"

"Five cans of ceiling white."

"Mildew, don't think I haven't noticed your little trips to the flea market."

"Hey, Rosie. Gimme a small grape juice and stick it on his tab."

"You're certainly a front-runner for the store detective job."

"One of everything."

"What a coincidence! You forgot my birthday and I forgot how to cook."

"One round-trip and one one-way."

"I told them I'd quit unless I got a bigger paycheck."

"How much to the airport if I drive?"

"I got you a four-slice toaster."

"Two coffees, one decaffeinated."

"Keep this in your room. We don't have a fire escape."

"Is this the first time you've
had your eyes tested?"

"I wouldn't sell this piece of
junk to my worst enemy."

"I just want to double-check your
order before I go. You did say
'Atlantic cod,' didn't you?"

"My name or the dog's?"

"This is the most expensive
perfume I could find without
my reading glasses."

"I wouldn't buy anything
else from the Amazon."

"Don't worry if this credit
card is reported stolen.
It's only my husband."

"If you find a pork chop in your
soup, it belongs to table nine."

"Quick...call a lawyer."

"I think it definitely
makes a statement."

"He's 70 million years old tomorrow."

"Will you stop grinding your teeth!"

"OK, OK... you can stay
out Saturday night."

"Last time I was here you said
I probably needed a cap."

"Grandpa, they've been arguing
all afternoon about who's
going to get your pool table."

"I'm prescribing two
coats of exterior latex."

"I just want to tell everyone that up until this moment, I've really enjoyed working here."

"I asked you what you wanted for lunch and you said, 'Surprise me.'"

"Helen, turn to Channel 22, 'World of Magic.'"

"I'b spled, I'b spill ab de benpisp."

"I never knew this had
a 'reverse' switch!"

"I can't adjust the air conditioning."

"You fell off the operating table."

"The bride made her own cake."

"Well I guess we can kiss a
promising radio career goodbye."

"We were made for
each other, Cybil!"

"I'll do your gallstones and
your wife's broken pelvis
for your left kidney."

"Hold on...something's
cutting into my side."

"Daryl...we don't need a meteorite!"

"Ladies and gentlemen...
the gride and broom."

"I told you not to plant it
too close to the house."

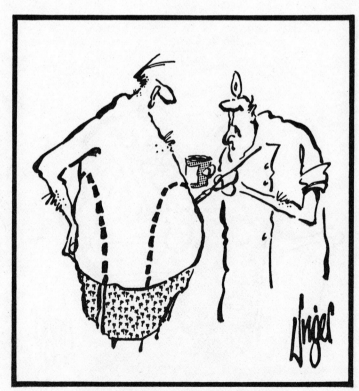

"We mark your ideal shape and
the laser does the rest."

"Can't you make yourself a cheese sandwich when I'm out all day?"

"Don't blame me! I told you to put it in the trunk."

"I had no choice. My wife thinks hunting is cruel."

"He likes to get a good
run at the mailman."

"What does that sound like to you?"

"I had a full head of leaves
when I was your age."

"No wonder that piano
tuner wanted 25 bucks!"

"Tell the manager I'm
declaring bankruptcy."

"I can't face the next thousand years
without my cup of coffee."

"When I told you to count
the pickled onions..."

"They feel comfortable.
What do they look like?"

"I use this one when it's raining."

"What's the paint-stripper of the day?"

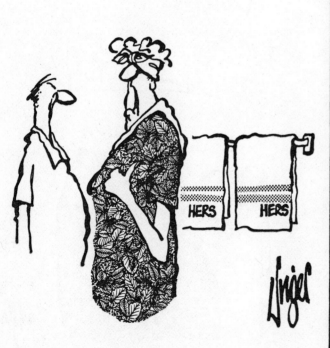

"Yours is under the sink."

"That quart of milk in the fridge expires at midnight."

"You the guy with a fly in his soup?"

"When you go to the bank tomorrow, you should find an extra $50,000 in your savings account."

"What's this made of...soap?"

"Your wife had a baby girl. I don't know if that makes you a daddy-mummy or a mummy-daddy."

"Any luck today, Betty?"

"I can't see him without an appointment!"

"Don't light that in here."

"The mail strike is over."

"Did you *have* to tell the newspaper reporters I was 57?"

"I'm so bad, I get a government grant not to paint anything."

"I asked that lawyer on the third floor what time he wanted me to clean his office and he sent me a bill for $65."

"He's badgering the witness, your honor."

"Eleven years ago he was told, 'Don't call us, we'll call you.'"

"I gotta pay tax on that
$5 Grandpa gave me!"

"Bernie, old boy...my wife doesn't
believe I was with you last night."

"I told you the sand was hot."

"It's just a back-up system
for your pacemaker."

"They're thinking of replacing
the $20 bill with a coin."

"Rather than an extra $20 a
week, how would you like to be
managing director of filing?"

"Henry, you've won a million dollars!"

"I'm *not* having 'Marlon.'"

"D'you wanna buy some 'equal-opportunity-Boy-Scout cookies'?"

"Got a hammer and chisel in avocado green?"

"You just ruined a perfectly good hole."

"Just show me the cheapest stuff in the store and I'll force myself to like it."

"I got 6 percent in math. Is that good or bad?"

"He always disappears when I want him to do the dishes."

"What happened to my sun screen?"

"Oh, no! We didn't get
our wake-up call."

"My kid ripped up the
ace of diamonds."

"Pizza's here."

"I don't mind pleading guilty,
your honor, if you'll grant me
immunity from prosecution."

126

"You say you've got a
ringing in your ears...."

"This is our new model,
'The Marriage Saver.'"

"How do you get these
little bottles in a typewriter?"

"Slow down at the next red light.
I wanna jump out."

"There's absolutely *nothing*
on TV tonight!"

"When I said 2 times 4 equals 6,
I meant after taxes!"

"Sure Dr. Butcher can do it
for $800....Have you seen
the size of his stitches?"

"The dollar's been weakening all
week....Got a hammer?"

"Can I have your hat?"

"I can't find Australia.
Are you sure it's on here?"

"How d'you expect me to remember
your birthday? I was only a year old."

"Number 87 . . . tomorrow
morning, 9 a.m."

"We ask for a $2 deposit
on the sausages."

"...with this ring I thee wed."

"I spilled my coffee
on the computer!"

"He always keeps me in the
style to which I'd become
accustomed...poverty."

"It says, 'How long before we land?'"

"Why don't we just call it quits and I'll cancel my next four trips?"

"I'll just let them help themselves."

"You're supposed to be at the church in 20 minutes."

"You're not even half as good as
my last driving instructor!"

"Has anyone seen my
other elastic stocking?"

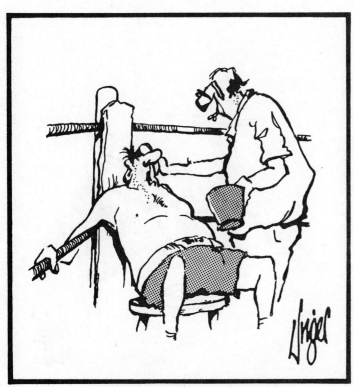

"Are you sure the referee didn't
hit me a couple of times?"

"That's the *third* time
you've agreed with him."

"Will you get a move on —
I got 200 sheep double-parked!"

"It dudn't get any better than this."

"Which way to the railway station...
both with sugar."

"When I shout 'waiter,' I expect
you to come immediately."

"He wants a second opinion, Ronnie."

"You call yourself a salesman!"

"Being stung by a jellyfish is a tough one, but I think we may be able to sue Jacques Cousteau."

"Go ahead. Make my day."

"You'd better go now. I'm not stopping halfway across the galaxy."

"If anything should happen to my nephew, Rodney, the bulk of my fortune will go to 'Big Louie.'"

"It's a movie about Houdini."

"Just say something about what it's like living here."

"I cannot drive with your foot hovering over the brake pedal!"

"Did you tell him he could
play with that paint?"

"How's your hay fever, Mother?"

"Who loaded this dishwasher?"

"I hope you're behaving yourself."

"It's just until the dessert trolley goes past."

"I told you not to rent that one."

"What have I got?"

"Have you heard that expression,
'You are what you eat'?"

"How does anyone get four aces
six times in a row?"

"I thought you said you
wanted it 'to go'!"

"Why don't you read
the rotten map yourself!"

"You won't be gaining another daughter, you'll be losing a son."

"How long does it take to walk down to the dispensary and get him a sleeping pill?"

"You didn't fill it up, did you?"

"I don't like it. He's stopped crying and started smiling."

"Guess who?"

"Take him straight down to X-ray."

"It's a bicycle roof-rack."

"I need both hands for turning!"

"Go and watch some lunatic behavior on TV. You're not old enough for this stuff."

"I wanted to ask you what you thought of gun control."

"He's a speed-reader."

"So then I said, 'The turning point in the women's liberation movement came when some guy invented the automatic transmission.'"

HERMAN by Jim Unger

THIS IS HOW IT STANDS...

I SPOKE TO THE JUDGE ABOUT PLEA-BARGAINING.

HE SAYS IF YOU PLEAD GUILTY, HE'LL GIVE YOU SIX MONTHS.

IF YOU PLEAD NOT GUILTY AND THE JURY FINDS OTHERWISE, YOU'LL GET TWO YEARS.

WHAT IF I PLEAD "VERY GUILTY"?

"I've already had three days
off sick this month."

"You ready?"

"Let me do the talking."

"What was that window cleaner shouting about?"

"Get a move on. I'm not paying $6 for another Frisbee."

"Go to sleep. Everybody has one foot bigger than the other."

"I told you I wanted that $800 electronic keyboard for my birthday."

"This is one of his earlier works."

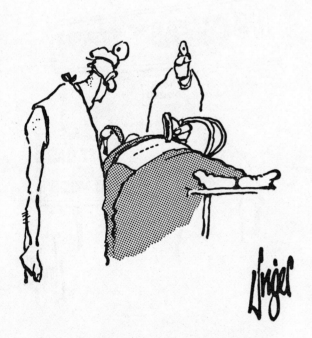

"Leave a clamp or something in me. I could really use the money."

"Has this dog been out today?"

"I should fire you, but I don't believe
in mixing business with pleasure."

"New airline strategy. All first-class
passengers have to have one."

"Don't keep changing your mind."

"I gave up all dreams of happiness
when I agreed to marry Henry."

"Can you send someone over to
fix the polygraph machine?
All the pens have broken off."

"You quit smoking *again*?"

"You're quite a puzzle, aren't you?"

"You sure think you know a lot
for a guy who grew up watching
black and white TV!"

"I think he's got
his mommy's mouth."

"Your wife stuck in the bath again?"

"I'm going to take you off
the nitroglycerine pills."

"Get your wife out of there, Mildew.
You're fired."

"I said, bring me a *pitcher* of water."

"She changed her mind."

"What exactly do you
do around here, Mildew?"

"The tow truck will be an hour. Why don't we rotate the tires?"

"I got a ticket for going the right way down a one-way street in reverse!"

"It doesn't have a reverse gear."

"He can't hold on forever."

"She's changed her nationality 14 times and still hasn't won anything."

"I need the front of a Ford and the back of a Toyota."

"Your skeletal structure can't support your weight anymore."

"I can't find that piece of steak anywhere."

"Say, ain't you that defector
from Mars I been reading
about in the paper?"

"It was just a bit of bad luck
that 11 of the 12 jurors
had their homes burgled."

"Sorry about the little accident,
sir. Do you still wish to
order something?"

"If I let you drive yourself home, are
you going to be turning left or right?"

"Use your fingers."

"You haven't the remotest idea what to get me for Christmas, have you?"

"I wish you wouldn't keep doing that."

"I said, 'Merry Christmas, Your Lordship. You can't take it with you.'"

"He just had a tooth
pulled by hypnosis."

"You can go home for Christmas."

"Mom, I'm going to bed now.
Wake me up Christmas morning."

"Will you please tell the court
if this is the man you saw
standing on the corner."

"Get the stuff wrapped. They must be asleep by now."

"Will you please say 'good night.' Our guests are leaving."

"If you don't mind me saying so, telling me that an old man with a beard is gonna come creeping in here tonight is not the best way to get me to fall asleep."

"Sign here."

164

TOY DEPT

"My sister wants to exchange this for a radio-controlled tank."

"Look in the brochure. See if it says it's dishwasher safe."

"We found him hiding in a laundry basket."

"So I said to him, 'Where is it written down that women should always be the one to look after a baby?'"

"What is it with your profession!
You're the 39th doctor to tell me
I'm a hypochondriac this year."

"This is your last chance, Steve."

"His idea of life in the fast lane is
going through the express checkout
with a can of prune juice."

"No offense, my dear, but I installed
a little electronic homing device
on the old suitcase."

"We only do dogs."

169

"Your wife's been watching
too many soap operas. You've got
ring-around-the-tube."

"I've got good news and bad news.
We found you a donor, but the guy
was 104 years old."

"This one's a big seller.
Makes you smell taller."

"When I said I wanted heavy-duty
shocks, I didn't mean the bill."

"And don't give me any of
those local anesthetics.
Get me the imported stuff."

"You'll need a wide-angle
lens for portraits."

"I'm gonna get you a Medic-Alert
bracelet just in case you're
ever found conscious!"

"Eventually, when we get more space,
we're gonna build them little houses
and give them real little lawn mowers."

"What's the number for
Dial-a-Prayer?"

"I've just proved I don't exist."

"He bought an exercise bike
and couldn't get it started."

"I'd better go...he's
waiting for his lunch."

"I remember when you could get
a bag of groceries for 30 cents."

"I can't remember: Are accountants
'left brain' or 'right brain'?"

"Your honor, my client pleads not
guilty to the charge of tailgating."

"After you finish writing that,
maybe you can find out who broke
into my apartment last week."

"If you're that tired, why
didn't you stay at home?"

"Would you prefer to eat inside?"

"*Never* trust a dog
that smiles like that."

"You never heard the expression, 'take a seat' before?"

"Ralphy...what did you use to get that new glue off your finger?"

"I was abandoned by my parents as a baby, and raised by a family of rabbits."

"He didn't know it was adjustable. He thought it was for vibrating massage."

"You'd better not play cards with your wife for a while."

"And when we come back, I'll be introducing you to someone who clearly demonstrates the falsehood that 'all men are created equal.'"

"He says he's developed a chemical dependency on three meals a day."

"Remember what you learned yesterday. You've got to sit up here behind the wheel."

"He says bullfighting is the only thing he's good at."

"Are you telling me your company expects you to sell cosmetics with a face like that?"

"The word on the street is that a guy named Hannibal is looking for a bunch of elephant trainers."

"This is my nephew, Eric. He wants to borrow that $100 you still owe me."

"This one lost the family fortune."

"So, did any of your other clients lose money on the stock market besides me?"

"I think we should move to a better neighborhood."

"That too tight?"

"Your scalp's very dry."

"Wait 'til you see his backhand."

"Is it OK if I run out and stick a few coins in the old parking meter?"

"I've been watching this quiz show for 15 years, and I've never once answered a question."

"386½..."

"Wake up. I'm lost."

"The phone company wants to know if they should bill us daily."

"We've put every piece of music ever recorded on one tape for $6.95."

"Is it the meat loaf again?"

"And another thing...I'm getting sick and tired of looking at that picture of Tom Selleck."

"Mom, look, we made Granddad smile!"

"No, no! custard, custard. ...Not Custer."

"Now don't go running off 'til
I find out where we are."

"How many times have I told you
about slamming that door!"

"You know I don't keep bath crystals
in the kitchen. This is Jell-O powder!"

"This our elephant trainer?"

"I was laid off work yesterday.
Wake me up in three weeks."

"And don't call me 'Stone Age.'
I'm Bronze Age."

"Get me a lawyer."

"If you *don't* mind, I prefer
being referred to as 'rear
animal impersonator.'"

"Take that off Dad's face. You've gotta get ready for school."

"Excuse me ... you're blocking the aisle!"

"When I was a little girl I used to be afraid of sliding down the drain."

"Make up your mind, Harold. Which one of us do you want to stay married to?"

"Don't turn around, and hand over the
keys to the monkey house."

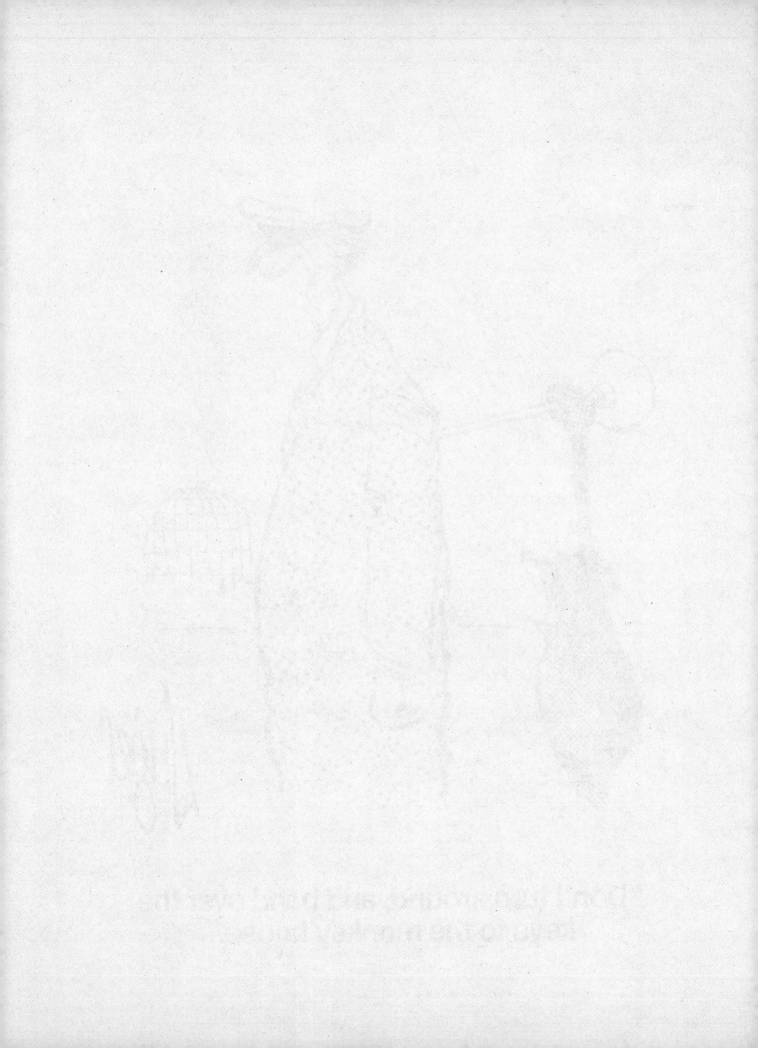

"The old methods are still the best."

"It's barely noticeable
from the outside."

"Just a few more minutes because
Daddy's on the night shift."

"Any idea where I left my razor?"

"It's very nice of your husband to
drive us all to the airport."

"Only *you* would be stupid enough to
park on the San Andreas fault!"

"Show me what to press
if I want to record a movie
after I've gone to bed."

"He wants to be a veterinarian."

"He says he's been swimming around in circles for three days."

"That guy in room 3401 wants to know when the elevator's gonna be fixed."

"I've quit my job at the bank."

"The main thing with a horse is you've got to make sure he knows who's the boss."

"Be careful on those basement stairs."

"I told you to call an electrician."

"On your mark...get set..."

"Grandma, can we borrow
these to make a tent?"

"Did you know you've got $34,000
worth of fire insurance on the
swimming pool?"

"This is an architect's office.
The chiropodist is next door."

"If I do happen to pick him out, what are the chances of him being held in custody long enough for me to emigrate?"

"I can let you have those for half price."

"Please fasten your seatbelt. We're expecting a little turbulence."

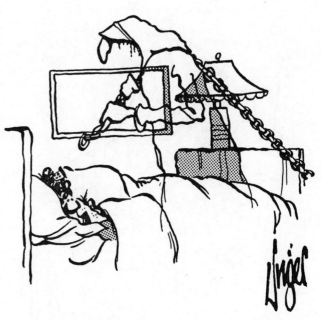

"Why would anyone rent us a nine-bedroom house for $200 a month?"

"I've been operating on a
malpractice lawyer all morning.
Look at my hands shaking!"

"Well, if it's the wrong number,
why did you answer the phone,
you idiot? Now I've lost my coin."

"He can't come to the phone.
He's busy watching television."

"Just a little exploratory surgery."

"Business or pleasure?"

"Is this the guy who
wouldn't eat the soup?"

"Grandpa, did you buy those pants
when you were a lot taller?"

"I never use this brand myself.
I find it makes my skin dry."

"It's not my fault if I thought
it was 'indigestion'!"

"Hi. I'm your new neighbor from
across the hall. I'm divorced, so
don't be surprised if I'm always
over here around mealtimes."

"Ear, nose, and throat!"

"So this is the best movie your
sister has ever seen."

"Can you type 40 words a minute?"

"You've got one hope...
reincarnation."

"His parents, grandparents, and
each of his great-grandparents
were all concert pianists."

"What are you, blind?
You hung it upside down!"

"Is that the jacket your grandson
bought you for your birthday?"

JUMBO HOT DOGS

"Don't play around with the seat."

"I ran out of the long buns."

"He says he leaves you everything
you left him... 38 bucks."

"Will you please mind your own
business and sit somewhere else?
I've had a very rough day."

"I told you to use your putter."

"Did you try the vertical hold?"

"You didn't have any money either
when you married Mom!"

"Let's face it, Edgar,
we're growing apart."

"That insurance salesman's
still out there!"

"What am I gonna do
about you, Phillips?"

"I definitely don't have
your size in beige."

"Now get up to your room until
you learn to act like a man."

"What about the ceiling in
the Sistine Chapel? I'm getting
sick of plain white."

"I told you not to order 'home fries'!
The chef lives 20 miles away."

"Got any 'get sick' cards?"

"Is he allowed to play with
knives? He's cut my hose!"

"Daddy, this is my new husband,
Bernie. He's a veterinarian."

"You're still cornering too fast."

"Do you *have* to fertilize
the lawn today?"

"I'm not gonna take any coffee breaks
this week so I can have Friday off."

"I was showing my sister-in-law how I
slammed his thumb in the car door."